EDGE BOOKS™

D0898424

Build It Yourself

BUILD YOUR OWN
FORT, IGLOO,
AND OTHER HANGOUTS

BY TAMMY ENZ

CAPSTONE PRESS
a capstone imprint

Edge Books are published by Capstone Press,
151 Good Counsel Drive, P.O. Box 669, Mankato, Minnesota 56002.
www.capstonepub.com

Books published by Capstone Press are manufactured with paper
containing at least 10 percent post-consumer waste.

Library of Congress Cataloging-in-Publication Data
Enz, Tammy.
    Build your own fort, igloo, and other hangouts / by Tammy Enz.
    p. cm.—(Edge books. Build it yourself)
    Includes bibliographical references.
    ISBN 978-1-4296-5436-4 (library binding)
    ISBN 978-1-4296-6261-1 (paperback)
1. Engineering—Juvenile literature. 2. Structural design—Juvenile literature.
3. Hiding places—Juvenile literature. I. Title.
TA149.E585 2011
624.1078—dc22
                                                    2010032205

Editorial Credits
Aaron Sautter, editor; Ted Williams, designer; Marcy Morin, project production;
    Eric Manske, production specialist

Photo Credits
All images from Capstone Press/Karon Dubke, except:
iStockphoto/Johnny Lye, 14–15, 16
Shutterstock/dabjola (shovel), 23, 24; DenisNata (tape measure), cover;
    HelleM (spray bottle), 22; M.E. Mulder (tape), 6, 7; PeppPic (safety pin),
    8, 9, 10; Roman Sigaev (nail), 11, 12, 13; Tihis (leaf), 17, 18–19, 20, 21;
    vilax (branch), 27, 31

Illustrations
Estudio Haus, 22–31

Design Elements/Backgrounds
Shutterstock/ARENA Creative, Eky Studio, Nanka, romvo, Vector

Capstone Press thanks Isaac Morin for his help in producing the projects
in this book.

Capstone Press also thanks George Sautter for the use of his garden for the
Edible Garden Fort project.

Printed in the United States of America in Stevens Point, Wisconsin.
092010   005934WZS11

Table of Contents

4 Build a Secret Hideout!

What do you need for the best summer fun? What makes a snowy day awesome? Your own secret hideout! And the best hideouts are the ones you can build yourself.

Want to build a colorful snow castle or a fort you can eat? You'll find instructions on these projects and more in this book. The materials you need may already be somewhere around your house. You'll be at home in your very own hangout before you know it.

Ask a friend to help you for extra fun. But remember that safety comes first. Be sure an adult helps you with dangerous tools such as saws and sharp knives. What are you waiting for? Let's get to work!

GATHER YOUR GEAR

Before you start building, take a few minutes to gather the tools listed below. Keep them organized in a toolbox so you can build your projects quickly.

MEASURING AND MARKING TOOLS

☐ pencil   ☐ ruler   ☐ tape measure

TIGHTENING AND LOOSENING TOOLS

☐ stapler   ☐ screwdrivers   ☐ hammer

☐ masking tape   ☐ electrical tape   ☐ hot glue gun

CUTTING AND SHAPING TOOLS

☐ drill   ☐ rasp   ☐ coping saw

☐ can openers   ☐ metal snips   ☐ scissors

☐ wire stripping tool   ☐ hand saw   ☐ pruning shears

☐ sandpaper   ☐ utility knife   ☐ wire snips

GRIPPING TOOLS

☐ needle-nose pliers   ☐ pliers

Soda Box Brick Fort

Did you know you can use empty soda boxes to build a fun and easy fort? When you're done, you can take it apart and make something completely different!

MATERIALS

- about 80 empty soda can boxes of various sizes
- masking tape
- paint

1

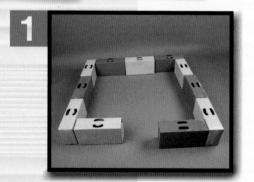

Seal the boxes shut with masking tape. Then paint them any color. Use 12-can boxes to lay out a rectangle three blocks long by three blocks wide. Leave out the middle block on one side for the door.

2

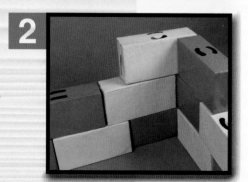

Stack another layer of blocks on top of the first. Overlap the blocks at the corners. Tape the layers together to make the fort stronger.

3

Keep stacking layers until the walls are at least six blocks high. Leave gaps between some blocks to use as windows.

Stack blocks in the same overlapping pattern to make the fort entry. You can use extra blocks to make the entry tunnel longer or give it a few bends.

4

5

Invite your friends over to enjoy your new fort!

TIP To collect enough boxes, ask friends and neighbors for their empty boxes. Keep an eye out for boxes at parties and picnics too.

Tie-Dye Tepee

This is no ordinary tepee! It's easy to build, and you can be sure nobody will ever have one like yours.

✂ MATERIALS

- 6 straight wood poles, 6 feet (1.8 m) long
- 1 or 2 packages of fabric dye
- 1 queen-sized white bed sheet
- rubber bands
- rubber gloves
- 6 to 8 safety pins
- heavy string

1 Prepare the fabric dye according to package directions. Bunch up different sized sections of the bed sheet and wrap rubber bands around them.

2

Put on the rubber gloves. Then dip the tied sections of the sheet in the fabric dye. Finally, wash and dry the tie-dyed sheet.

3 Lay three poles together on the ground. Tie them together with heavy string about 6 inches (15 cm) from one end.

4 Stand the poles up and spread them out to form a tripod. Then tie each of the remaining poles between the first three. This will create a cone-shaped frame for the tepee. Make sure the connections are tied tightly so the frame is secure.

5

At the top of the frame, pin the sheet together to hold it in place. Pin the sheet together about every 4 inches (10 cm) along the overlapping cloth.

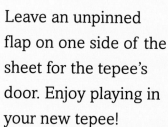

6

Leave an unpinned flap on one side of the sheet for the tepee's door. Enjoy playing in your new tepee!

TIP Instead of tie-dying the sheet, try using fabric paints or glitter to give your tepee a creative touch.

Edible Garden Fort

What could be cooler than a fort you can eat? This hideout gives you privacy and shade—and you can snack on it! Grab your gardening gloves and get ready to build a green getaway.

✂ MATERIALS

- 2 sheets of wood lattice, 4 feet (1.2 m) wide by 8 feet (2.4 m) long
- thin, strong wire
- 4 large nails

- 4 pieces of wood, 3 inches (7.6 cm) wide by 1 foot (.3 m) long by ¾ inch (2 cm) thick
- pole bean seed packets
- string

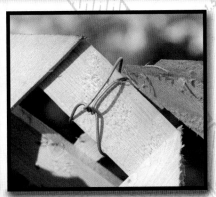

1

This hideout works best if you start in the spring. Find a sunny spot at the edge of a garden. Prop the lattice pieces against each other horizontally to form an upside down V shape. Use wire to tie the lattice together at the top about every 12 inches (30 cm). Then place the frame on the soil where you want the fort to be.

⚠ *Keep Building!* 〉 11

Pound a large nail into the end of one piece of wood. Place the wood through an opening in one corner of the lattice frame near the ground. Be sure the nail faces out. Drive the wood into the ground to anchor the lattice. Repeat this step for the other three bottom corners.

Plant the bean seeds along the outside of the fort walls according to package directions. Water the seeds regularly. Then sit back and watch your fort grow.

As the vines grow, you may need to train them to grow up the fort walls. Gently tie the vines to the lattice with string.

When the beans are ripe, enjoy your tasty snacks in the shade on a hot summer day!

5

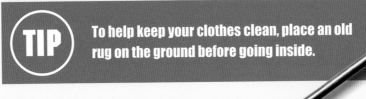

TIP To help keep your clothes clean, place an old rug on the ground before going inside.

Umbrella Tent

Umbrellas can do a lot more than protect you from the sun and rain. Try out this cool project to make an easy and unique tent.

 MATERIALS

- 1 large golf umbrella
- 1 old queen-sized bed sheet
- several safety pins
- PVC pipe, 6 inches (15 cm) wide by 5 feet (1.5 m) long
- old newspapers
- shovel

Find a level spot of ground. Use the shovel to dig a small hole about 12 inches (30 cm) deep. Place the PVC pipe in the hole. Refill the hole around the pipe and stomp on the dirt to pack it down.

Open the umbrella and place the handle into the PVC pipe. Stuff crumpled newspaper into the pipe around the umbrella handle to make it stable.

Measure the distance from the point of one umbrella rib to the ground. Measure and mark this distance on the bed sheet. Use scissors to cut the bed sheet lengthwise to the measured width.

3

4

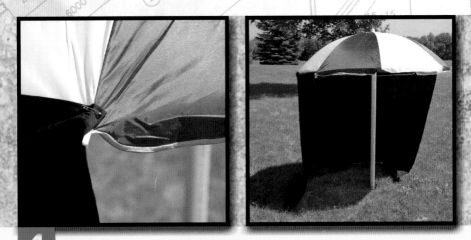

Use a safety pin to attach one corner of the sheet to one umbrella rib. Repeat this step at each rib. Wrap the fabric around the umbrella as you go.

5

When you get back to the first rib, trim off any extra fabric.

6

Crawl through the open flap to enjoy your new tent!

 TIP Use clothes pins to keep the tent flap closed when you're inside.

Leafy Hut

If you're hiking without a tent, this leafy hut can give you plenty of shelter. You can also use it to create a woodsy hangout in your own backyard.

MATERIALS

- 6 straight, clean branches, 1 inch (2.5 cm) thick by 6 feet (1.8 m) long
- several long, leafy branches
- thin, strong wire
- 2 short, pointed sticks
- 12 sturdy branches, 2 to 3 feet (.6 to .9 m) long
- 3 feet (.9 m) of string

1

Find a level spot of ground 6 to 8 feet (1.8 to 2.4 m) wide. Clear it of rocks and sticks. Tie one short, pointed stick to the end of the string. Push the stick into the ground at the center of the hut's location. Tie the second pointed stick to the other end of the string. Use the stick to mark out a 6-foot (1.8 m) wide circle around the center stick.

2

Push the thick end of one long branch 6 inches (15 cm) into the ground at the edge of the circle. If the ground is too hard, dig a small hole and place the branch into it. Then fill it with dirt and stomp the dirt tightly around the branch. Place a second long branch into the ground directly across the circle from the first branch.

3

Bend the two long branches toward each other. Overlap the ends by several inches and tie them together with wire to form an arch shape.

4

Repeat steps 2 and 3 until the circle is divided into six equal parts. Tie all the arches together at the top to make a dome-shaped frame.

TIP Wire can be sharp to work with. Be sure to wear gloves to protect your hands.

5

2'

Find six sturdy branches about as long as the distance between the ribs of the dome. Use wire to tie each of these branches between the ribs about 2 feet (.6 m) above the ground.

6

Repeat step 5 and tie more branches about 4 feet (1.2 m) above the ground. The frame of your hut should now be solid and stable.

4'

Be sure to leave a space for a door so you can crawl through. Once the hut is stable, you may need to move a stick up to make the door higher.

7

Door

8

Gather several long, leafy branches. Work around
the hut frame, weaving the leafy branches in and
out vertically between the ribs. Finally, weave
more leafy branches horizontally through the
vertical branches. Then move your camping gear
inside and enjoy your cool, shady hideout!

TIP If you have lots of clay soil nearby, you can turn
this into a clay hut. Mix clay with water until it's
pasty. Plaster the clay all over the leaves inside
and out to form a solid dome. Then let it dry.

Colorful Snow Castle

You'll be the king of the neighborhood in this backyard castle. It will take some muscle to build, but it's worth it. Get some friends together and get to work!

✂ MATERIALS

- lots of wet, sticky snow
- 1 large garbage can
- plastic 5-gallon (19-l) bucket
- snow shovel
- 1 spray bottle
- water
- food coloring
- 1 piece of plywood, 2 feet (.6 m) wide by 4 feet (1.2 m) long

Find a spot with deep, well-packed snow. Measure and mark out a 7- by 7-foot (2.1- by 2.1-m) square. This will be the outline of the castle. Use your heel to mark the outline in the snow.

1

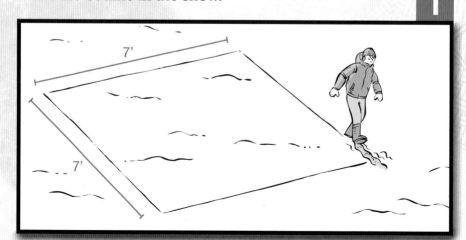

2

Dig a trench about 2 feet (.6 m) wide by 2 feet deep on the outside of the square. This trench will be the castle's moat.

3

Use the snow from the trench to fill the garbage can. When the can is full, turn it upside down on each corner of the square to make the castle towers. Ask an adult to help lift the can if it's too heavy.

4

Gently empty buckets of snow between each tower to make the castle walls. Be sure to leave an opening in one wall for the door.

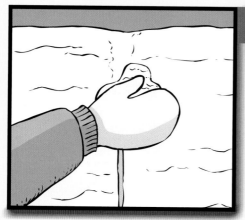

5

Pack snow into the gaps in the walls. The extra snow will make the walls solid and stable.

6

Fill the spray bottle with water. Add several drops of food coloring and shake it to make colored water.

7

Spray the castle with the colored water. Use several different colors if you want. Get creative and try spraying different designs on the walls of your castle.

8

Place the board across the moat as a drawbridge. After crossing the bridge, prop it up against the doorway to keep intruders out. Invite your friends to come over for some fun in your private frozen fortress!

TIP When the castle is finished, you can dig out the floor inside the castle. Use the snow for snowballs to help defend the castle while you stay safe inside.

Glowing Igloo

Long ago, the Inuit people lived, slept, and even cooked in snow houses. Gather some friends and learn to build your very own igloo. Then huddle inside to feel like an arctic adventurer!

✂ MATERIALS

- lots of hard-packed snow
- snow shovel
- string
- short stick
- small trowel
- spray bottle
- 2 or 3 battery-powered candles
- plastic bin, 9 inches (23 cm) wide by 16 inches (41 cm) long; 9 inches (23 cm) deep

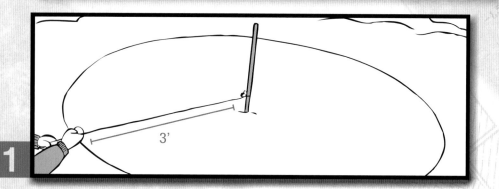

1

Find a level spot of ground where the snow is at least 1 foot (.3 m) deep. Once you have a good spot, measure out a 3-foot (.9-m) piece of string. Tie one end to a stick. Push the stick into the snow at the center point of the igloo's location. Stretch out the string and walk around the stick to mark out a 6-foot (1.8-m) wide circle.

2

Pack snow into the plastic bin with the shovel to make a snow block. Empty the bin onto the outline of the igloo. Gently shake it to remove the block.

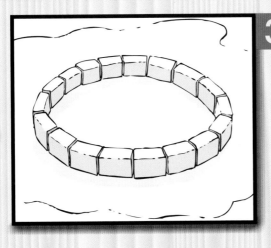

3

Repeat step 2 until you've placed blocks around the entire circle. Place the blocks as close to each other as possible.

4

Use snow to fill in the gaps between the blocks. If the snow doesn't stick, use a spray bottle to wet the blocks first. Then pack snow between them.

Place a second row of blocks on top of the first. Keep the second row about 1½ inches (3.8 cm) inside the front edge of the first row.

5

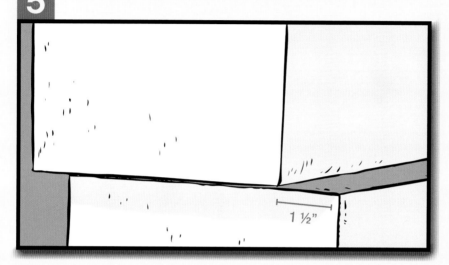

Pack snow in the gaps between the blocks as in step 4. Do this inside the igloo too. Repeat steps 5 and 6 to add three or four more levels to the igloo.

6

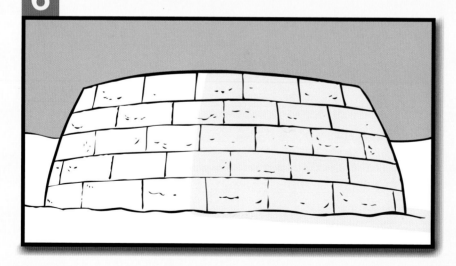

7 After a few levels are in place, you may not be able to step over the walls. Remove part of the first two or three rows of blocks to make a door.

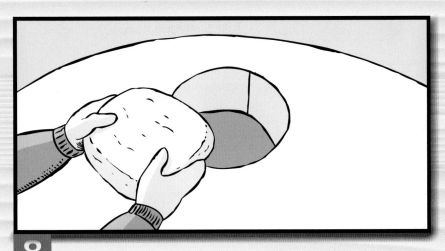

8 Keep placing rows of blocks until the dome is closed. Use your shovel to trim the final block to the correct size and shape for the top of the igloo. You may need some friends or an adult to help you put the final block in place.

9

Make more snow blocks to create a tunnel to the door. Make the tunnel walls 4 or 5 rows high and about 15 inches (38 cm) apart. Set more blocks on top of the walls to make the tunnel roof. Pack snow between all the blocks to make the tunnel stable.

15"

10

Use the small trowel to cut two or three small, 4-inch (10-cm) square windows in the walls of the igloo. This will allow light and fresh air to flow into your hideout.

11

Level out the windowsills. Place a battery-powered candle in each window hole. This will light your igloo and make it glow in the dark at night.

Your igloo is done! Invite your friends inside and imagine you are arctic explorers in your new snowy hangout.

12

TIP You can try having a sleepover in the igloo. Put some waterproof sleeping bags on the floor. The closed dome will help keep you warm and toasty inside.

READ MORE

Popular Mechanics. *The Boy Mechanic: 200 Classic Things to Build.* New York: Hearst Books, 2006.

Stiles, David and Jeanie Stiles. *Treehouses and Other Cool Stuff: 50 Projects You Can Build.* Salt Lake City, Utah: Gibbs Smith, Publisher, 2008.

Strother, Scott. *The Adventurous Book of Outdoor Games: Classic Fun for Daring Boys and Girls.* Naperville, Ill.: Sourcebooks, 2008.

Internet Sites

FactHound offers a safe, fun way to find Internet sites related to this book. All of the sites on FactHound have been researched by our staff.

Here's all you do:

Visit *www.facthound.com*

Type in this code: 9781429654364

 Check out projects, games and lots more at **www.capstonekids.com**